THE LITTLE FROG'S GUIDE TO LIFE

MAYBELL EEQUAY

summersdale

THE LITTLE FROG'S GUIDE TO LIFE

An Hachette UK Company
www.hachette.co.uk

Summersdale Publishers
Part of Octopus Publishing Group Limited
Carmelite House
50 Victoria Embankment
LONDON
EC4Y 0DZ
UK

www.summersdale.com

This FSC® label means that materials and other controlled sources used for the product have been responsibly sourced

MIX
Paper | Supporting responsible forestry
FSC® C016973
www.fsc.org

The authorized representative in the EEA is Hachette Ireland, 8 Castlecourt Centre, Dublin 15, D15 XTP3, Ireland (email: info@hbgi.ie)

Printed and bound in China

ISBN: 978-1-83799-473-1
eISBN: 978-1-83799-657-5

TO ALL OF THE FROGS OUT THERE
WHO ARE TRYING THEIR BEST TO
MAKE SENSE OF THIS BEAUTIFUL
AND WEIRD WORLD WE LIVE IN.

A SPECIAL THANK YOU TO MY MOM
AND JUJU FOR HELPING ME FIND MAGIC,
INSPIRATION AND LESSONS IN
EVEN THE HARDEST MOMENTS.

CONNECTING WITH YOURSELF

TAKE CARE OF YOURSELF THE SAME WAY YOU WOULD CARE FOR SOMEONE YOU LOVE. ALL IMPORTANT RELATIONSHIPS REQUIRE SOME LEVEL OF NURTURING, AND YOUR RELATIONSHIP WITH YOURSELF IS NO DIFFERENT.

WHEN YOU ARE TRYING TO WORK ON YOURSELF OR MAKE IMPROVEMENTS IN YOUR LIFE, IT'S IMPORTANT TO TAKE IT SLOW AND TO BE PATIENT. BY SLOWLY INCORPORATING ONE OR TWO NEW THINGS INTO YOUR LIFE AT A TIME, YOU ARE MORE LIKELY TO STICK WITH THEM THAN IF YOU TRY TO CHANGE SEVERAL THINGS ALL AT ONCE.

GENTLY MONITOR THE WAY THAT YOU SPEAK TO AND THINK ABOUT YOURSELF. IF YOU FIND THAT YOUR SELF-TALK TENDS TO BE UNKIND, HARSH OR EVEN HATEFUL, TRY TO ACKNOWLEDGE AND ADJUST THOSE THOUGHTS IN THE MOMENT TO SOMETHING MORE COMPASSIONATE.

IT MIGHT FEEL SILLY AT FIRST BUT, OVER TIME, YOUR RELATIONSHIP WITH YOURSELF CAN COMPLETELY TRANSFORM.

I'm going to be
nicer to you

IF YOU FEEL LIKE EVERYTHING IS FALLING APART, REPEAT TO YOURSELF, “EVERYTHING IS GOING TO BE OKAY.” TRY TO LET YOURSELF REALLY FEEL AND BELIEVE THOSE WORDS BECAUSE, MORE OFTEN THAN NOT, IN THE BIG PICTURE, EVERYTHING WILL BE OKAY.

IN THE MORNING, TRY TO LET YOURSELF FULLY WAKE UP AND GET READY FOR THE DAY BEFORE CHECKING YOUR EMAILS, TEXTS AND SOCIAL MEDIA. YOU MIGHT BE SURPRISED AT HOW MUCH CLEARER YOUR MIND FEELS IF YOU DON'T CHECK YOUR PHONE UNTIL AFTER YOU'VE EASED INTO YOUR DAY.

No!

TRY NEW THINGS AND BE OKAY WITH NOT BEING GOOD AT THEM.

Reality:

IF YOU ARE FEELING ANXIOUS OR STRUGGLING WITH BEING PRESENT, TRY USING YOUR SENSES TO HELP PULL YOU BACK INTO YOUR BODY.

* EAT A MEAL WITHOUT DISTRACTIONS AND REALLY FOCUS ON WHAT YOU ARE EATING. WHAT DOES IT TASTE LIKE? WHAT DO YOU LIKE ABOUT IT? HOW MANY FLAVOURS CAN YOU IDENTIFY?

* WASH YOUR WRISTS OR FACE WITH COLD WATER.

* TAKE YOUR SHOES OFF AND STAND ON THE GRASS.

* IF YOU HAVE SOMEONE WITH YOU WHO YOU FEEL COMFORTABLE WITH, ASK THEM TO LOOK INTO YOUR EYES UNTIL YOU START LAUGHING.

* EAT A PIECE OF SOUR CANDY.

* CLOSE YOUR EYES AND FOCUS ON YOUR BREATHING. WHAT CAN YOU SMELL WHEN YOU INHALE?

IF YOU ARE IN THE TRENCHES OF DEPRESSION AND HAVING A HARD TIME GETTING OUT OF BED, TRY SITTING OUTSIDE FOR A BIT. IT MIGHT NOT SEEM LIKE MUCH, BUT GETTING FRESH AIR CAN MAKE A BIG DIFFERENCE TO YOUR DAY AND IT MIGHT EVEN INSPIRE YOU TO GO FOR A WALK.

This is actually
kind of nice

DO YOU HAVE ANY BELIEFS ABOUT YOURSELF THAT MIGHT BE HOLDING YOU BACK FROM LIVING A HAPPIER LIFE? LIMITING BELIEFS ARE DIFFERENT FOR EVERYONE BUT MIGHT LOOK SOMETHING LIKE:

✷ BELIEVING THAT YOU ARE UNLOVABLE

✷ BELIEVING THAT YOU ARE AN UNLUCKY PERSON

✷ BELIEVING THAT YOU AREN'T SMART

✷ BELIEVING THAT YOU AREN'T GOOD ENOUGH

✷ BELIEVING THAT YOU ARE UGLY

AT SOME POINT IN YOUR LIFE YOU MIGHT HAVE THOUGHT OR BEEN TOLD ONE OF THESE THINGS AND YOU MAY HAVE INTERNALIZED IT AS A FACT... BUT IT ISN'T! YOU CAN CHALLENGE THESE BELIEFS AND, WITH A LITTLE PRACTICE, YOU CAN LET GO OF THEM ENTIRELY.

SPEND TIME WITH YOUR TREASURES AND HEIRLOOMS. TAKE THEM OUT, DUST THEM OFF, HOLD THEM. WHAT FEELINGS DO THEY EVOKE? WHY ARE THEY SPECIAL TO YOU? SOMETIMES SPENDING TIME WITH OUR LITTLE EARTHLY TREASURES CAN FEEL LIKE VISITING AN OLD FRIEND.

IF YOU CAN LEARN TO ENJOY YOUR OWN COMPANY, THEN YOU WILL ALWAYS HAVE SOMEONE TO DO THINGS WITH THAT YOU LIKE BEING AROUND. EMBRACING MOMENTS OF SOLITUDE CAN OPEN THE DOORS TO A WHOLE NEW OUTLOOK ON LIFE.

KEEP A JOURNAL. JOURNALLING CAN HELP YOU TO PROCESS FEELINGS, REDUCE STRESS, TAKE NOTE OF DAY-TO-DAY LIFE AND CREATE A PLACE TO HOLD YOUR MEMORIES. YOUR JOURNAL CAN ALSO RECORD YOUR DREAMS AND WISHES, AND IT CAN BECOME A TOOL TO EXPLORE YOUR HEART AND MIND TO SEE WHAT YOU ARE LONGING FOR.

HAVING THE ABILITY TO LOOK BACK ON YOUR THOUGHTS, FEELINGS, MEMORIES, DREAMS AND WISHES YEARS DOWN THE LINE CAN BRING YOU CLOSER TO YOURSELF THAN YOU EVER IMAGINED. YOU MIGHT EVEN FIND THAT SOME OF THE THINGS YOU CURRENTLY HAVE IN LIFE ARE THINGS YOU ONCE WISHED FOR.

FIVE JOURNAL PROMPTS

TAKE INVENTORY OF YOUR LIFE:

* WHAT DO YOU LOVE? INCLUDE BOTH BIG AND SMALL THINGS.

* WHAT ARE YOU LACKING?

* WHAT'S BRINGING YOU DOWN?

* WHAT LIFTS YOU UP, OR WHAT WOULD LIFT YOU UP?

* WHAT WOULD YOU LIKE TO CALL INTO YOUR LIFE OR MAKE MORE TIME FOR?

WHAT WOULD
YOU DO IF YOU
WEREN'T AFRAID?

WHAT IS CURRENTLY IN YOUR LIFE THAT YOU ONCE WISHED FOR?

THIS WEEK,
I WANT TO
WORK ON...

____________________.

WHAT DO YOU WANT YOUR LIFE TO LOOK LIKE ONE YEAR FROM NOW?

CONNECTING WITH PEOPLE AND THE WORLD AROUND YOU

IF YOU WANT TO ADD A LITTLE SWEETNESS INTO THE WORLD, WRITE A LETTER TO A STRANGER, WISHING GOOD THINGS FOR THEM, AND LEAVE IT ON A PUBLIC BENCH.

IF YOU HAVE A LITTLE EXTRA CASH, MAYBE EVEN ADD IN A CONTRIBUTION TOWARDS A COFFEE OR TREAT.

Hello

IF AN ANIMAL, PLANT OR INSECT KEEPS SHOWING UP IN YOUR LIFE, TAKE NOTE OF IT. WHAT CHARACTERISTICS DOES IT HAVE? ARE THERE ANY LESSONS THAT YOU COULD PULL FROM IT? NOT EVERYTHING HAS TO BE A SIGN OR A TEACHER, BUT IF SOMETHING KEEPS SHOWING UP AND FEELS SIGNIFICANT, IT MIGHT BE.

Thanks for the ride
No problem

DON'T BE AFRAID
TO ACCEPT HELP
WHEN YOU NEED IT.

Wait up!

IF YOU HAVE A LONG-DISTANCE FRIEND, LOVED ONE OR ACQUAINTANCE, ASK TO BECOME PEN PALS WITH THEM. RECEIVING HANDWRITTEN LETTERS FROM PEOPLE YOU CARE ABOUT IS A TRUE TREASURE AND CREATES SOMETHING FOR BOTH OF YOU TO LOOK FORWARD TO.

IF YOU LIKE SOMETHING ABOUT SOMEONE, TELL THEM (EVEN IF THEY ARE A STRANGER)! SO OFTEN WE ADMIRE THINGS ABOUT PEOPLE BUT NEVER SAY THEM ALOUD, AND YOU NEVER KNOW HOW MUCH SHARING YOUR THOUGHTS MIGHT MEAN TO THEM.

Thanks
I like your
boots

DON'T UNDERESTIMATE HOW HEALING IT CAN BE TO SPEND TIME QUIETLY SITTING BY WATER, LOOKING AT THE NIGHT SKY, OR WALKING IN THE WOODS.

SOME OF THE MOST INTERESTING, KIND AND SPECIAL PEOPLE YOU WILL EVER MEET ARE THOSE WHO HAVE SEEMINGLY UNREMARKABLE LIVES. TRY NOT TO OVERLOOK THEM, BECAUSE YOU MIGHT MISS OUT ON SOME OF THE BEST PEOPLE YOU'LL EVER KNOW.

ALWAYS BE TEACHABLE.

THERE ARE SO MANY WAYS
TO CONNECT WITH PEOPLE
AND THE WORLD AROUND YOU!
FIND OUT WHEN METEOR SHOWERS
ARE VISIBLE WHERE YOU LIVE;
PUT A BLANKET DOWN ON THE GRASS
AND WATCH THE CLOUDS; IF YOU
SEE A BEE STRUGGLING, GIVE IT A
LITTLE SUGAR WATER; HOLD THE DOOR
OPEN FOR THE PERSON BEHIND YOU;
VOLUNTEER IN YOUR COMMUNITY;
GET TO KNOW YOUR NEIGHBOURS.
LIFE IS FULL OF MAGIC AND SURPRISES.

LITTLE REMINDERS

WHEN YOU LOOK FOR
BEAUTY IN THE WORLD,
YOU WILL FIND IT.

YOU HAVE MANY MORE
“BEST DAY EVERS”
AHEAD OF YOU.

YOU DON'T NEED
TO BE EXCEPTIONAL.

WHO YOU ARE,
AT YOUR CORE,
IS A KIND OF MAGIC
THAT NO ONE
CAN REPLICATE.

YOU ARE NOT
YOUR WORST
MOMENTS.

YOU CAN GROW AND
EVOLVE WITHOUT
ABANDONING YOURSELF.
SOMETIMES TRYING
NEW THINGS LEADS
TO FINDING YOURSELF,
WHICH IS SOMETHING
THAT MOST OF US
HAVE TO DO OVER
AND OVER AGAIN.

NOT EVERY CHAPTER OF YOUR LIFE HAS TO BE NOTEWORTHY OR EXCITING.

DOWNTIME IS IMPORTANT.

IT'S OKAY IF YOU DON'T HAVE A "DREAM JOB". WHAT YOU DO TO SURVIVE DOESN'T NEED TO DEFINE WHO YOU ARE AS A PERSON. YOU ARE SO MUCH MORE THAN WHAT YOU DO TO PAY YOUR BILLS.

TAKE TIME TO BE ASTONISHED.
MAGIC CAN BE FOUND IN THE
MOST UNEXPECTED PLACES.

WHEN YOU MAKE A DECISION THAT IS RIGHT FOR YOU, IT DOESN'T ALWAYS FEEL GOOD – BUT THAT DOESN'T MEAN YOU DID THE WRONG THING.

GIVE BIG FEELINGS TIME. PROCESSING YOUR EMOTIONS, ESPECIALLY THE STRONG ONES, CAN HELP YOU GAIN A BETTER UNDERSTANDING OF WHAT YOU ARE FEELING AND HOW TO RESPOND.

DISCOMFORT ISN'T ALWAYS A BAD THING; IT IS OFTEN ESSENTIAL TO GROWING.

SOME OF THE BEST PARTS OF YOUR LIFE WILL COME FROM STEPPING INTO THE UNKNOWN.
I am brave and good things will come from this

THE
UNKNOWN

REMEMBER, YOU HAVE COME A VERY LONG WAY AND OVERCOME MANY THINGS IN THIS LIFE. CHERISH THE PEOPLE WHO MAKE YOU LAUGH AND EMBRACE EVEN THE SMALLEST MOMENTS OF JOY. IT'S EASY TO BECOME HARDENED BY THIS WORLD, BUT IT'S BRAVE TO HOLD ON TO THE PARTS OF YOU THAT ARE TENDER. THE WORLD DESPERATELY NEEDS MORE TENDERNESS.

YOU ARE MAGIC
PERSONIFIED.

... and don't
forget it!

ABOUT THE AUTHOR

Maybell Eequay is a Minnesota-based artist who works in many different mediums. Born and raised in the breathtaking St. Croix River Valley, Maybell draws a lot of inspiration from her childhood homelife as well as her love of vintage children's books and knickknacks. Growing up in a creative household and as the daughter of two artists, Maybell has been making art since she was old enough to hold a pen. Today, she enjoys making art that has a vaguely nostalgic feel paired with tender messages and light humour.

Find Maybell on Instagram at
@maybell.eequay

ALSO BY MAYBELL EEQUAY:

THE LITTLE FROG'S
GUIDE TO SELF-CARE

978-1-83799-101-3

THE LITTLE FROG'S
GUIDE TO SELF-CARE
CARD DECK

978-1-83799-519-6

THE LITTLE FROG
JOURNAL

978-1-83799-693-3

THE LITTLE FROG
NOTEBOOK

978-1-83799-736-7

Have you enjoyed this book?

If so, find us on Facebook at **Summersdale Publishers**, on Twitter/X at **@Summersdale** and on Instagram and TikTok at **@summersdalebooks** and get in touch.

We'd love to hear from you!

www.summersdale.com